∵ STORIES FROM ∵
THE BIBLE

© 1997 Grandreams Limited.

Published by
Grandreams Limited
435-437 Edgware Road, Little Venice,
London, W2 1TH.

Printed in Hong Kong.

C O N T

THE OLD TESTAMENT

E N T S

THE NEW TESTAMENT

The Garden of Eden

God made a beautiful garden in the East. He planted trees and plants that were lovely to look at. The Tree of Life and the Tree of Knowledge of Good and Evil were also planted in the garden.

This was the Garden of Eden, and Adam, the first man, was put in the garden to look after it. He could eat any fruit except for that of the Tree of Knowledge.

One day, while Adam slept, God took one of his ribs and made a woman. She was called Eve.

The most cunning creature in the garden went up to Eve one day.

"Is there any fruit here you are not to eat?" hissed the snake.

"We may eat any fruit," said Eve, "except for the fruit of the Tree of Knowledge. That fruit will kill us."

"It will not kill you," said the snake. "God knows that if you eat the fruit you will see both good and evil, and you will be wise and as powerful as he."

Eve took some fruit to eat, and gave some to Adam.

As they ate, they realised they could see more clearly. They saw that

all your life," he said.

God turned back to Eve. "You will suffer great pain during childbirth," he told her. "You will turn to your husband for happiness."

God then turned to Adam. "You ate fruit forbidden to you. You must leave the Garden of Eden forever, and work to survive. There will always be weeds to clear when you grow your crops. And when you die you will return to earth."

With that, God banished Adam and Eve from the Garden of Eden, and placed a guardian angel at the gate to protect it.

they wore no clothes. Immediately they gathered fig leaves to make clothes.

They then hid among the trees.

God walked in the garden later, looking for Adam.

"Where are you?" he called.

"We are here," called Adam from the tree. "We do not wish you to see us without clothes."

"Who said you needed clothes?" cried God. "Have you eaten of the Tree of Knowledge."

"My wife, Eve, gave it to me," said Adam.

"What have you done?" God asked Eve.

God then turned to the snake. "You are cursed and shall stay on your belly

Noah's Ark

Adam and Eve had many children, who in their turn had many children.

Generations of man moved about over the world.

One day, God looked down at the people on the earth and did not like what he saw. He saw evil in their hearts. He was sorry he had ever created man.

"I will get rid of the people and all

other living creatures," said God. "They have spoiled the earth I made."

God looked around one last time to see if there were any good people. He found one man who pleased him. Noah was a good man who believed in God. He had three sons - Ham, Shem and Japheth.

God looked again at the evil people, and then called to Noah, "I am going to rid the World of all evil people.

I will destroy them with a great flood. But I want you, Noah, to build a great boat, an Ark, from gopher wood. You must paint it inside and out with pitch to waterproof it. There will be three decks, one door and one window."

God gave Noah further instructions and Noah hurried to do as God said.

"Come wife, come sons," called Noah. "We have much to do."

With his sons Noah built the great Ark as God had described.

People laughed to see them working on such a great boat.

When the Ark was finished, Noah carried out God's instructions and gathered together a male and female of every one of the creatures on the earth and they were led onto the Ark.

"The rain will come in seven days," God had told Noah, and so he and his sons now had to work hard to gather enough food and water for all the creatures on the Ark.

"It will rain for forty days and nights," God had also told Noah. On the seventh day, Noah boarded the Ark and closed the door on himself, his family and all the noisy creatures.

Just as God had said, the next day it began to rain.

The waters rose and rose, lifting the Ark and all its inhabitants. It continued to rain for the next forty days and nights.

The waters filled the rivers, then the valleys. They covered the plains and then covered the mountains.

Every living thing on earth was drowned. The only survivors were those on the Ark.

After forty days and nights of rain, God made a wind blow across the land and the rain stopped.

Gradually the waters began to drop and after 150 days the Ark came to rest on a mountain. The water still dropped and after five months, Noah sent out a raven and then a dove to find dry land. The dove returned.

Another seven days passed and Noah released the dove again. This time she returned with an olive leaf in her beak.

"There is dry land somewhere!" cried Noah. "It will not be long now before we are able to leave the Ark."

Seven days later Noah sent out the dove again. This time she did not return.

"The waters are gone," said Noah. "The flood is over!"

He then opened the door to see the dry land.

God then spoke to Noah. "Release all the creatures on the Ark and go on to the earth with your family."

Noah and his family walked out on to the earth and all the animals that followed were now in a clean land.

Noah and his family were very happy and they built an altar.

"This is a new beginning," said God. "I will never bring a flood again."

To show His promise, God created a rainbow in the sky. And ever since, a rainbow has appeared at the end of a rainstorm to remind everyone of God's promise.

The Tower of Babel

After Noah and the great flood, many generations were born and lived on the earth.

There were many people, but they spoke but one language. Everyone understood everyone else.

People moved across the great plain of Shinar and decided to settle there.

"Let us make bricks," said the people. "Then let us make a tower, a tower so high that it will reach the heavens. Let us make a name for ourselves across the earth so that none shall forget us."

God went down to the city and saw the tower. "Behold," he said. "They are a people, with one language and they have only just started. There is no limit to what they could achieve. I will confuse their language so that they cannot understand each other."

God went among the people and gave each person a new language to speak.

The people looked at each other in astonishment. Nobody could understand anyone else! How could they build their tower? No instructions could be given or understood.

The tower was then abandoned and the people moved on.

The tower was called the Tower of Babel, where God made men babble in strange tongues.

Lot's Wife Looks Back

One of the greatest men in the Bible was called Abraham. He was chosen by God to be the leader of the Hebrew nation. But first God had work for Abraham to do.

One day, God told Abraham that he had decided to destroy two wicked cities called Sodom and Gomorrah.

Abraham was very distressed when he heard this for his nephew, Lot, was living with his family in Sodom. Abraham begged God not to destroy Sodom. God told Abraham that if ten good people could be found in that city he would not destroy it.

Then God sent two of his messengers to Sodom to try and find ten good people. They met Lot at the gate of his house and Lot offered them a night's lodging.

Some time later, many angry men arrived at Lot's house demanding that the two strangers should be handed over to them. Somehow they must have learned that the men had come to do them harm.

Lot refused to hand over the two strangers and the furious men grabbed hold of Lot. The two messengers pulled Lot back into the house and struck blind all those who had attacked him.

Then one of the messengers spoke to Lot: "We are here to try and find ten good people living in Sodom. If we cannot, God will destroy Sodom. Take your family and leave the city at once. If you stay here, you may be in deadly peril." So Lot, his wife and daughters made ready to leave Sodom.

"Go to the hills and do not look back whatever happens," Lot and his family were warned.

Lot and his family sped away from Sodom. They had not gone far before they heard the thunder of destruction smashing the city to pieces. All who live there were killed for there were not ten good people living in Sodom.

Lot's wife had fallen behind her husband and daughters. At the sudden noise, she turned and looked back. She was at once changed to a pillar of salt. Lot and his daughters, though, escaped the terrible anger of God.

Abraham and Isaac

God told Abraham that his wife Sarah would have a baby, Isaac. "How can I be a mother at my age?" she had laughed.

God heard her laugh. "Why does Sarah laugh?" he asked Abraham. "Sarah will have a son as I have said." A year later, as promised, Sarah

had a baby boy and he was called Isaac.

Abraham was one hundred years old and Sarah was ninety years old.

Isaac grew happily, and while he was still young, Abraham took him on a journey to visit the surrounding lands.

One day, God called out, "Abraham!"

"Here I am," replied Abraham.

"Take your son, your only son whom you love dearly and take him to the land of Moriah. Offer him there as a burnt offering on one of the mountains. I shall tell you which one."

The next morning, Abraham arose early and called his son and two young men who would act as guards on the journey.

"Come saddle the ass," said

Abraham. "We travel to Moriah."

Abraham cut some wood to take, then mounted his ass and led the way to the land of Moriah.

They travelled for two days and on the third day Abraham raised his eyes and saw the land of Moriah ahead.

"You two must wait here with the ass until our return," Abraham told the two young men. "Isaac and I must go on ahead." Abraham took the wood from the ass and the knife.

"Father," called Isaac, in a puzzled voice.

"Yes, my son," said Abraham.

"Father, you have wood for the fire, the knife to sacrifice, but where is the lamb for the burnt offering?" asked the boy.

Abraham took Isaac by the hand and started to walk. "God will provide the lamb for the offering," he told Isaac.

They arrived at the place God indicated, and Abraham built an altar there.

Then Abraham took hold of his son and tied him with some rope until he could not move. With tears in his eyes he picked up his son and put him on the altar. He then took up the knife, ready to sacrifice his son.

But an angel called out to him, "Abraham! Do not harm your son! We know now that you fear God as you were ready to sacrifice your only son. Behold!"

Abraham looked up to see a ram caught in a thicket. He rushed up and freed it and put it on the altar in place of his son.

The angel called a second time, "You and your descendants are indeed blessed."

Jacob and Esau

There were many generations of people after Noah and his wife and their family.

A man named Abraham had a son called Isaac. He was happily married to a girl called Rebekah. But Rebekah was sad, because she had no children.

Isaac prayed to God and his prayer was answered. Rebekah found that she was pregnant, with twins. The babies used to struggle inside her, and she asked God the reason.

"There are two nations inside you," explained God. "Two peoples will be born and they will be divided. One will be stronger than the other. The younger will be served by the elder."

The time came for the babies to be born, and when they were born the first baby to come out was very hairy. He was called Esau. The second baby held his older brother by the heel, and he was called Jacob.

The boys grew up happily, both very different in character. Esau loved the outdoors, and Jacob was quieter and stayed close to the tents. Isaac's favourite son was Esau, while Jacob was his mother's favourite.

One day, Esau returned from hunting, tired and hungry. His brother was stirring a stew over the fire.

Esau sat down next to Jacob. "That smells delicious," he said. "I'm starving. Do give me some."

"You can have some," said Jacob, "if you give me your rights as the oldest son."

"My rights?" said Esau. "I'm famished, and my birthright can't feed me. Yes, you can have it - only give me some of that stew!"

So Esau sold his birthright.

The years passed, and Isaac was growing old. His eyesight was failing, and he knew that he would soon die. He called his oldest son to him.

"Esau, I want you to go hunting and whatever you kill, will you cook for me in a tasty way? I will then give you my blessing."

Esau fetched his bow and quiver and set off.

Rebekah had heard her husband talking to Esau, and she called for Jacob.

"Quickly," she said. "You must kill a goat, and I shall cook it just the way your father likes. He has sent Esau to kill some game and plans to give him his blessing. You must go in his place and receive the blessing."

"But what if he touches me?" asked Jacob. "My brother is a hairy man. Father will not be fooled."

"Let me worry about that," said his

22

mother. "You kill the goat."

While the meal was cooking, Rebekah cut some strips of goat skin and attached them to Jacob's arms and legs. She put Esau's clothes on him so that he would smell like his brother. The she sent Jacob into his father with the stew.

"That was very quick," said Isaac in surprise.

"God must have helped me," said Jacob, in a deep voice, something like his brother's.

"Come here. Come closer," said Isaac. "Let me feel that you are indeed Esau."

Jacob went closer to his father, and Isaac stretched out his hand to touch Jacob's arm. He could feel the fur, and smell Esau's clothes and decided it was Esau.

He gave his younger son his blessing saying that he would be head of the family.

Jacob hurried away, not wanting to be there when Esau returned.

Esau returned with a deer, and cooked it to his father's taste. He then took the stew into his father's tent.

As soon as Isaac heard his son's voice he knew that he had been tricked.

"Oh, my son!" he cried. "I have given my blessing to your brother! You are too late. He tricked me into giving him what was rightfully yours! I'm sorry, my son."

Esau was furious, and cried out, "I will kill him! He has already taken my birthright for a bowl of stew, and now he has your blessing!"

Rebekah heard the shouting and ran to Jacob.

"You must leave," she told him. "Go to my father and stay there. Find a wife among his people. I will reach you somehow when it is time to return."

So Jacob left his father's home and went to his mother's family far away.

The Coat of Many Colours

Jacob lived among his mother's people for many years, and when he finally returned to his home he had two wives, Leah and Rachel.

Jacob was now called Israel. He made his home in Canaan. He had twelve sons. His first wife, Leah, had six sons - Reuben, Simeon, Levi, Judah, Issachar and Zebulun. Her maid had two sons, Gad and Asher. Rachel, his favourite wife, had two sons, Joseph and Benjamin, but she died shortly after having Benjamin. And her maid had two sons, Dan and Naphtali.

After Isaac died, Jacob lived on in Canaan. Joseph, his eleventh son, was his favourite. When he was seventeen years old, his father gave him a coat of many colours. His brothers were very jealous, as none of them had received such a gift from their father.

After a while, they found that they could hardly talk to him without wanting to hate him.

One night, Joseph had a dream, and he told his brothers about it in the morning.

"I dreamed that we were out in the fields, gathering the sheaves of corn. My sheaf of corn suddenly stood up straight and tall, and all your sheaves began to bow before it!" he told his brothers.

His brothers were not too pleased to hear this, and their hatred grew deeper for Joseph.

"Do you mean to say that you will be a leader, and we will have to bow to you?" they asked bitterly.

A few nights later, Joseph had another dream, and the following morning he told his family. "The sun, moon and eleven stars were bowing down before me," he said.

This time his father was angry.

25

"Are you saying that your mother and I as well as your brothers will be bowing to you?"

His brothers were even more angry.

One day, the brothers were looking after the family's sheep and goats near Shechem. Jacob called Joseph to him.

"Go to your brothers and see how the flocks are. Then come back and tell me."

As Joseph approached his brothers, they could see him coming. He wore his multi-coloured coat.

"Here comes the dreamer," said one brother.

"What does he want?" asked another.

"Probably another dream he's had," said a third.

"Whatever it is, I don't want to hear it," said the first brother.

"Then let's do something about it," said another brother. "Let's kill him and leave him in a pit for the wild animals to find."

"No! You can't do that!" cried Reuben. "Throw him in a pit to teach him a lesson, but don't kill him!" Reuben decided that he would go back later and release his brother.

Joseph came up to his brothers, and they seized him and tore his coat off and threw him in a deep pit.

They then sat down to eat. As they ate, a cloud of dust appeared on the horizon. It was a caravan of merchants.

"This could solve our problem," said Judah, as he stood to greet the merchants. "Let's sell Joseph to the merchants. They can take our problem away with them."

The brothers agreed, and Joseph was sold for twenty shekels of silver. Joseph was taken to Egypt to be sold as a slave.

"What can we tell our father?" one brother asked.

"Let's say that wild animals took

27

him," another suggested.

A goat was killed, and blood was put on the coat. This was taken back to their father.

"Wild animals must have taken him," said Joseph's brothers. "This is all that was left."

Jacob was heartbroken and could not be comforted.

Joseph was taken to Egypt and there he was sold as a slave to Potiphar, the captain of the Pharoah's guard.

God watched over Joseph, and saw that he succeeded in all he did. Soon he was in charge of the household, but one day Potiphar's wife accused him of attacking her.

Nobody believed Joseph was

innocent, even though he had been loyal. He was taken to Pharoah's prison.

Again God watched over Joseph.

One day, two important prisoners were brought in - Pharoah's baker and his butler. The men had displeased the Pharoah.

One morning, the two men looked very unhappy.

"What is wrong?" asked Joseph.

"We have both had a dream," said the baker. "You know we Egyptians like to understand our dreams and there is no one here to help us."

"Tell me your dreams," said Joseph. "I'm sure God will help me to understand them."

The butler told his. "I dreamed there was a vine, with three branches. Each budded, flowered and grapes appeared as I watched. I then squeezed juice into Pharoah's cup.

"In three days from now, you will be restored to your position and will again place Pharoah's cup in his hand. Please remember me, for I am innocent of any crime."

The baker, hearing that the butler's dream promised good fortune, eagerly told his dream.

"I had three baskets of bread on my head, and the top one was for Pharoah. But birds flew down and ate from the basket."

"You also will be taken from here in three days, but you will be taken out to a tree and hung there for the birds to peck at you."

The baker was horrified.

Three days later it was Pharoah's birthday. He released the butler and restored him to his former position, putting the cup in his hand.

The baker was taken out and hung, as Joseph had said.

The butler forgot his promise to Joseph.

Joseph remained in prison.

Joseph and Pharoah

Two years passed, and one night Pharaoh had two dreams.

"I was by the Nile and seven fat cows were grazing. Seven thin cows came up to them and ate them but remained thin," he told his advisers the next morning, waiting for an explanation.

"In the other dream, seven fat ears of corn were growing on one stalk. Seven thin ears then grew, and ate the seven fat ears, but the thin ears remained thin," said Pharaoh.

No one could give any explanation to Pharaoh. "I need to know their meaning," Pharaoh told his butler.

"There is someone who may be able to help," said the butler. "There is a young man, Joseph, in your prison who told the baker and I the meaning of our dreams when we were there, and he was absolutely right."

Pharaoh ordered that Joseph be brought to him.

"Will you tell me the meaning of my dreams?" Pharaoh asked.

"I can't, but God can," said Joseph, and he listened carefully as Pharaoh repeated his dreams.

"God has sent you two dreams with the same message," said Joseph. "The seven fat cows and seven fat ears of corn signify seven good harvest years, when there will be plenty of grain for all. But the seven thin cows and seven thin ears of corn mean this time of plenty will be followed by seven years of famine. You must prepare by putting away grain each year, ready for the times of hardship to come."

"But who can do such a task?" asked Pharaoh, and then he realised that Joseph would be the perfect person, as God was obviously with him.

Joseph was immediately dressed in the finest linens and given the task of saving and storing the grain for the years of famine to come.

Joseph became Pharoah's Prime Minister, and for the next seven years of bounty organised the gathering of a fifth of all grain. It was stored in great warehouses in the larger cities. Eventually even Joseph did not know how much was stored, only that there would be sufficient for the seven years of famine.

Those seven years began, and again Joseph was kept busy with the distribution of the grain, selling it to be sure that all had their fair share.

The famine spread, and soon reached Canaan.

Jacob heard that there was grain to be bought in Egypt and sent his ten oldest sons to Egypt to buy some. He kept Benjamin near him, as he could not bear the thought of losing Rachel's other son.

Joseph was in charge of selling the grain, and immediately recognised his brothers, although they did not know him.

"Where are you from?" he asked, already knowing the answer.

"Canaan," they replied, kneeling before Egypt's prime minister.

Joseph suddenly remembered his own dream of the sheaves of corn.

"Who are you then?"

"We are brothers, the sons of Jacob in Canaan. Our youngest brother is at home with our father, and another brother is dead."

Joseph felt strange to be told he was dead by his brothers.

"I say you are spies," said Joseph. "You will be put in jail. You cannot leave here until you promise to bring your youngest brother here to prove what you say is true."

The ten brothers were put in jail, and the third day Joseph went to them.

"One of you shall stay here, and the rest can return with the grain you have bought. But you must return with your youngest brother," Joseph told them.

Joseph ordered that Simeon be put in the jail, and the remaining brothers set off for their home. They also found that unknown to them, their money had been replaced in the sacks, by Joseph's orders.

"Now we will be thought of as thieves!" they cried and they told Jacob what had happened.

"You cannot take Benjamin!" cried Jacob. "I have lost Joseph and Simeon, I will not lose Benjamin!"

The famine continued, and gradually the grain bought in Egypt was used. "You must go back to Egypt and buy more," said Jacob to his sons.

"We cannot go without Benjamin," they reminded him.

"How does he know about Benjamin?" asked Jacob.

"He asked us many questions, about home, you and Benjamin," said the brothers.

"Well then, you must go back and take Benjamin with you," said Jacob at last. "But you must promise on your lives to bring him back."

Judah replied, "We will return, or the blame will be mine."

"You must go with gifts - honey and almonds. And also twice as much money. Say that there was a mistake last time you went. May God bring you and your brothers home safely."

The brothers arrived in Egypt, and Joseph saw that Benjamin was with them.

He gave orders that they should be taken to his house to stay. "Is your father well?" Joseph asked, and was happy to hear that Jacob had been well when they left.

The following morning the brothers' sacks were filled with grain. Their money was also returned, and a silver cup was placed in Benjamin's sack.

They set off for Canaan, but after a few hours were stopped by Joseph's guards.

"You have stolen from our master," said the guards.

"Why should we steal?" asked the brothers. "Our money has been returned to us again. If one of us has stolen, then he shall be killed and the remainder will remain as slaves!"

The sacks were searched, and there in Benjamin's sack, was the silver cup.

The brothers were horrified, but turned around and headed back for the Egyptian city.

Once more before Joseph, they threw themselves on their knees. "What can we say?" they cried. "We must be your slaves!"

"You can all go except the guilty one," said Joseph. "He must be a slave."

Judah spoke up. "Take me instead, my lord," cried Judah. "If we return without Benjamin, our father will be heartbroken. He has already lost one son. Let me stay!"

Joseph could stand it no more.

"Clear the room!" he cried. "Not you," he added to the brothers.

The servants and soldiers left the room, puzzled at the events.

"I am Joseph," he said simply.

Benjamin looked, and saw that it was true.

"I am your brother," said Joseph. And he hugged Benjamin, and the brothers all saw it really was Joseph.

"You sold me to the merchants, and I was sold here, and God has looked after me while I have been here."

The brothers hugged each other, delighted with their reunion.

"I was sent here to prepare for the famine," explained Joseph. "Enough grain was stored to ensure that there would be plenty for all. Return to Canaan, and bring back our father to live in Egypt. You will be given land in Goshen."

The brothers returned to Canaan with their happy news about their brother Joseph.

"I will go to Egypt," said Jacob, "and see my son before I die."

God spoke to him that night, telling Jacob that he would make a great nation of him in Egypt. "I will stay with you in Egypt and lead you out again."

Jacob and his enormous family made the long journey to Goshen where Joseph and his father were finally reunited.

Jacob died seventeen years later, and his body was taken back to Canaan to be buried with his forefathers.

Moses in the Basket

A new king reigned in Egypt who had not heard of Joseph or of his help in time of famine. He worried about the increasing number of Israel's people and set them to work, building and working in the fields.

They became slaves to the Egyptians.

Still the people flourished so the Pharaoh gave orders that all boy babies should be thrown in the Nile.

An Israelite woman was to have a baby. When the baby was born, it was a boy. The woman did her best to keep the baby hidden. She did not want him to be thrown into the Nile.

But after three months, he was growing fast and soon making too much noise to keep him secret.

Finally, she made a basket of bulrushes and waterproofed it with mud. She took the basket with the baby inside, down to the river. She went to a spot where she knew the Pharoah's daughter often bathed.

"Stay by the basket," she told her daughter Miriam. Miriam sat by the basket for a while, and then heard voices. The princess was walking up the bank. Miriam quickly hid, away from the basket.

The baby began to cry. "Find that poor baby!" the princess told her servants.

The servants found the baby boy in the basket and took him to the princess.

"Oh, the poor baby," said the princess. "He must be one of the Hebrew babies. We must find someone to look after him. He will not be cast into the Nile."

At that point, Miriam threw herself from her hiding place.

"I know someone to care for him," she said running up to the princess.

"Quickly, bring the woman here," said the princess, still holding the baby.

Miriam ran off to fetch her mother.

"I want you to take care of this baby, as if he were your own child," the princess told Miriam's mother. "I shall pay you, and you shall live under my protection. When the baby is grown to a boy you must bring him back to me."

Miriam's mother was delighted, and several years later, she took the boy back to the princess.

"I shall call you Moses," the princess told him, as she formally adopted the young boy as her son, "because I took you from the water."

When Moses was returned to the princess, his mother had one last thing to tell him. "You are an Israelite, my son. Never forget your people."

In the palace, he was dressed in the finest robes, but he never forgot that he was born an Israelite, not an Egyptian. As he grew he saw how his people were treated as virtual slaves by the Egyptians.

One day, he saw an Israelite being badly beaten by an Egyptian. He followed the Egyptian, and when he was sure no-one was looking, he killed the man and buried him in the sand.

The next day he saw two Israelites fighting and ran to separate them. "Who do you think you are?" asked the man who had started the fight. "You cannot judge us. Or will you kill me the way you killed the Egyptian?"

Moses was horrified. "Does everyone know?" he thought. "What if Pharoah hears?"

Pharoah did hear of it, and he gave orders for Moses to be killed.

Moses ran away. He stayed in Midian, where he married.

In Egypt, the Pharoah died. Another Pharoah took his place, and still the people of Israel were badly treated.

They called on their God to help them. He heard and remembered his promise to Jacob.

The Flight from Egypt

God chose Moses as his messenger, to talk to the Israelites and to Pharoah.

"I shall send you to Pharoah, and you must ask him to let my people go."

Moses went with his brother Aaron, and Pharoah refused to let the Israelites go.

God turned the water of the Nile to blood, but Pharoah would not let the people go.

God sent plagues of frogs, gnats and flies. Only the land of Goshen, where the Israelites lived, was spared.

Still Pharoah would not give in.

A plague on the Egyptians' animals followed. Those of the Israelites were untouched.

The people of Egypt were then affected by boils on the skin, but still Pharoah would not listen.

God then made a storm of hail fall upon the land of Egypt - it killed everything that was not under shelter. Only the land of Goshen was spared.

The flax and barley were ruined in the fields, but the wheat had not yet sprouted.

God then sent a plague of locusts to strip every green plant growing in Egypt. Not a tree, bush or plant remained.

But Pharoah would not give in.

God then spoke to Moses.

"I shall now send the worst plague on the people of Egypt," he said. "Then Pharoah will let you go. Tell Pharoah and his people that I am going to kill the firstborn of every living creature, man or beast, but the people of Israel will not be harmed."

Pharoah was given this warning by Moses, but he still would not let the Israelites leave Egypt.

God then told Moses what the people of Israel should do.

"This month shall be the first month of the year for you, from now on. On the tenth day of this month, every household shall choose a lamb. On the fourteenth day in the evening, the lamb shall be killed in every household, and some of the blood shall be put on the lintel and doorposts of the house. Then roast the lamb and eat it all that night. Any remaining must be burned before morning. Then you will be clothed and staff in hand, for that night I shall pass through the land and will kill all the firstborn. The blood on the lintel and doorposts will tell me to pass over that house and spare those inside.

"You will keep this day as a feast day, and from this day from the fourteenth to the twenty first day of this

first month, you will eat only unleavened bread in the evening."

Moses told the people of Israel to prepare the lambs for the Passover. They did as God commanded, and on the fourteenth night God passed through Egypt slaying the first born of all the creatures. No household was unaffected - from prisoners in the dungeons to the mighty Pharoah. No people of Israel were harmed.

The next morning, Pharoah called Moses and Aaron to him.

"You may go," he told them as the sounds of wailing and crying echoed in the palace.

The people of Israel then left Egypt, some six hundred thousand men, women and children after 430 years in that country. They took with them the bones of Joseph, as he had asked.

God led them with a pillar of cloud by day, and a pillar of fire at night, that they might travel day and night.

God led them to the shores of the Red Sea.

"Pharoah will pursue you," he told

Moses. "But I will be victorious over Pharoah and his armies. The Egyptians will know that I am the Lord."

Meanwhile Pharoah had realised that he had let his workforce go. He called for six hundred picked charioteers, and all the chariots of Egypt. He then pursued Moses and the Israelites, almost catching up with them at the Red Sea.

The people of Israel were terrified. They could see the dust thrown up by the wheels of the chariots.

God then spoke to Moses. "Stretch your cane out over the waters. Tell the people to go forward. The waters will divide and the people will go through the sea on dry land."

The pillar of cloud moved behind the people of Israel and the darkness confused the Egyptian army so they did not catch up with them that night.

Moses stretched his hand out over the waters of the Red Sea, and the waters divided. The people of Israel began their walk across the riverbed, with high walls of water to their left and right.

God watched as Pharoah and his army followed the people of Israel onto the dry path. He made the path muddy and boggy, difficult for the chariots to follow.

Moses then stretched his hand over the waters, and the sea returned to normal, drowning and destroying all those of Pharoah's army that had followed the Israelites onto the path.

When the Israelites saw the drowned Egyptian soldiers, and that God had saved them, the people of Israel rejoiced.

Joshua at Jericho

Joshua was now the leader of the twelve tribes of Israel and it was to him that the people looked. Joshua would lead the people across the river Jordan into Canaan.

"This land is yours, as promised to Jacob and Joseph," God told Joshua.

The first city they saw was Jericho. Joshua sent two spies into the city to see how prepared it was.

Jericho was a great walled city, and was very old.

The two spies were in the city and nearing the city walls when they met a woman called Rahab. She knew there was something different about them and she took them to her home.

Word reached the King of Jericho that there were two men of Israel in the city and that they were at the house of Rahab. He sent soldiers to capture the men, but Rahab hid the two spies on her roof.

"Bring out the two men of Israel," the soldiers ordered Rahab. "They have been sent to spy on us and the city."

"Two men were here earlier," said Rahab. "I don't know where they were from. They left here - just before the city gate closed for the night. You may

still catch them on the road if you go quickly."

The soldiers left, hurrying to the city gate. The gate was opened for them and they rushed for the fords of the River Jordan. The gate closed quickly behind them.

Rahab returned to the roof. "We have heard of your coming for many

months, and how you have defeated armies, kings and cities. It is said that your God has given you this land. We heard of the parting of the Red Sea and the defeat of Pharoah. There is no courage in any man in the city as it seems that all fall before you. You will now take Jericho. Swear to me by your Lord, that I have treated you well, that I have helped you. When you come to Jericho again, treat me well and show mercy to me and my family."

"We promise, if you do not tell of us, we will show mercy to this house," said the two men.

Rahab was happy with their promise, and taking them to a window in her house that was in the city wall, let them down to the ground below.

"Hide in the hills for three days," she advised the two spies. "The soldiers will return and you can then go on your way."

The two men gave Rahab a scarlet cord.

"Tie this to the window in the city wall," said the men. "Bring all your family to this house and keep them here. Don't let anyone go beyond the gate or they shall be killed. Stay in the house and you will all be safe."

Rahab tied the scarlet cord to the window.

The two spies did as Rahab advised and hid in the hills for three days until all signs of pursuit had gone. They then returned to Joshua with news of how scared the people of Jericho were.

Joshua and the tribes of Israel crossed the Jordan into Canaan and

camped near Jericho.

God gave Joshua his instructions for taking the city of Jericho.

On the first day, Joshua ordered that seven priests, each bearing a ram's horn trumpet would walk in front of the army around the city of Jericho.

"You will walk around the city once, and you must not say a word until the day I tell you to shout," Joshua told the soldiers.

The priests led and the vast army followed. Not a word was spoken while the horns were blown continuously.

On the second day, the priests, blowing the trumpets, walked once around the city.

The priests led the army around the city for six days. On the seventh day, the priests were to lead the army seven times around the city.

"The priests will make a long blast on the trumpets and then the people of Israel shall shout," Joshua told the army. "The city will then be yours. All within the city shall be destroyed, except for those in the house of Rahab, who helped our men while in the city."

The priests and the army marched and on the seventh passing of the city gate, the trumpets blew one long blast and the people of Israel gave a great shout.

The great walls of the city fell down flat, and the army rushed into the city, killing all before them, men and women, young and old, oxen, sheep and asses.

Joshua called the two spies to him. "Go to the house of Rahab, and bring her and her family out as you promised. Take them somewhere safe near our camp."

The two young men did as they were ordered, and Rahab and her family were brought safely out.

The city of Jericho was then burned to the ground.

Deborah the Prophetess

After the death of Joshua, the people turned from God and began to worship Baal and Ashtaroth. God punished them by allowing armies to succeed against them.

God sent judges to help them, but each time a judge died the people returned to their evil ways.

Jabin, King of Canaan, ruled Israel cruelly for twenty years. His army commander was Sisera. Deborah sent for Barak from Kedesh.

Deborah, a prophetess, was judging Israel at this time.

"The Lord commands you to gather ten thousand men from the tribes of Naphtali and Zebulun at Mount

Tabor. Then God will draw out Sisera to meet you by the river Kishon and give him into your hand."

"If you will go with me, I will go," said Barak.

"I will go," replied Deborah. "You will receive no glory. God will deliver Sisera to a woman."

Barak summoned the men from the tribes of Naphtali and Zebulun, and with ten thousand men went to Mount Tabor. Deborah accompanied them.

Sisera was told of Barak's activities and gathered his nine hundred chariots, and all his men and led them to Kishon.

Barak led out his ten thousand men, and the Lord led Sisera and his chariots straight onto the swords and arrows of Barak's soldiers. Sisera fled. Barak chased after and all the men of Sisera's army were killed. Not one lived.

Sisera ran and arrived at the tent of Jael, the wife of Heber. There was peace between the family of Heber and King Jabin.

"This way," said Jael. "Fear not."

Sisera went into the tent, and Jael hid him beneath a rug.

"A drink, please," said Sisera.

Jael opened a skin of milk for him and poured a drink.

"If anyone comes tell them no one

is here," said Sisera, as Jael hid him again.

Jael then took a wooden tent peg and hammer, and drove the peg into Sisera's temple as he slept. There he died.

Barak approached the tent.

"Wait," called out Jael. "The man you seek is in the tent."

On that day God helped to subdue Jabin, and he helped the people of Israel drive into Canaan until Jabin was destroyed. There was then peace in the land for forty years.

The Trumpets of Gideon

Gideon was one of the judges chosen by God to help the Israelites, who had strayed and worshipped Baal. He pulled down the altar to Baal.

A Midianite army crossed the Jordan. The spirit of God entered Gideon, and he sounded his trumpet and all his people followed him. Messengers went all through Manasseh, calling the people to follow.

Then Gideon said to God. "If you will deliver Israel by my hand, see I am laying a fleece on the threshing floor. If the fleece is wet with dew, and the ground is dry, I shall know you will deliver Israel by my hand." The next morning, Gideon was able to wring out a bowlful of dew from the fleece, while the ground was still dry.

Gideon and his army camped beside a spring. The Midianite camp was just to the north.

The Lord said, "There are too many to deliver Israel. They will think they did it themselves."

"Let those who are afraid go home," Gideon said to the army. Twenty-two thousand departed, and ten thousand remained.

"There are still too many," said God. "Take them down to the water and I will test them."

The people went down to the water and began to drink.

"Set aside all those who sip from their hands," said God. They numbered three hundred. The remainder knelt down to the water.

"With these three hundred, I will deliver Israel," said God. "Send the others home."

Gideon led the three hundred to the Midianite camp.

That night God sent Gideon, with his servant Purah, down to the enemy camp. "Hear what they say," said God.

The army of the Midianites was vast. Gideon heard a man telling of a dream. "A cake of barley bread tumbled into the camp and flattened a tent."

"This is the sword of Gideon. God has given Midian and the army into his hand," said his friend.

Gideon returned to the camp, praising God.

He split his army into three groups, and gave them all trumpets and jars holding torches.

"Watch me and do as I do," Gideon told the army. "When I blow the trumpet, blow the trumpets on all sides and shout, 'For the Lord and for Gideon!'"

Gideon took his company to the camp and there they blew their trumpets

and smashed their jars holding the torches and trumpets high.

"A sword for the Lord and for Gideon!" they cried, and they held their ground all around the camp while the Midianite army cried out and fled.

Samson's Riddle

One day an angel appeared before the wife of a man named Monoah and told her that she would have a son. The baby was called Samson, and his mother, as told by the angel, never cut his hair.

When Samson was grown, he went to Timnah and saw the daughters of the Philistines.

"I have seen the daughters of the Philistines, and I wish to marry one of them," he told his parents.

"Choose among your own people," begged his parents, not realising that God wanted Samson to marry the girl.

"She pleases me," said Samson. "I will marry her."

Samson went with his parents to Timnah. Samson went alone to the vineyards and was attacked by a lion. But God was with Samson, and Samson killed the lion with his bare hands. He did not tell his parents what happened.

Samson continued on and met the girl. He liked her, and after a while he returned to marry her. On his way, he went to the vineyard and found the lion skin there. Inside he found a swarm of bees and honey. He scraped out some honey and went on his way, eating honey.

The wedding feast was to last seven days, and Samson would follow Philistine tradition by giving garments to the guests for coming to the feast.

But first he said, "I have a riddle. If you can solve it by the end of the feast, I shall give you the garments. If not, you all shall give me garments."

"Tell us," said the young men.

"Out of the eater came something to eat," said Samson. "Out of the strong came something sweet."

After three days, the guests still had no idea. They went to Samson's new wife.

"Get the answer," they said, "or we will burn down your father's home."

Samson's wife wept before him. "You cannot love me. You have given my countrymen a riddle and you have not told me the answer."

"I have told no one the answer," said Samson.

His wife pleaded and wept, and on the seventh day Samson relented and told her. She immediately told her countrymen.

That evening, the men said to Samson, "What is sweeter than honey? What is stronger than a lion?"

"You have taken the answer from my wife!" shouted Samson, and he went into town and killed thirty men and returned with their garments for the thirty guests. In a fury he returned to his parent's home.

David
and King Saul

Saul was King over all Israel but had turned from God and did not do as he was commanded.

God therefore spoke to his prophet, Samuel, "Go to Jesse of Bethlehem, I have chosen a King from among his sons."

"I come to sacrifice to the Lord," said Samuel once at Bethlehem.

Jesse and his sons were invited. Seven sons passed before Samuel. "This is not the one the Lord has chosen," said Samuel of each son.

"Are all your sons here?"

"The youngest is keeping the sheep," said Jesse.

"Send for him," said Samuel.

When David arrived God said, "Anoint him, this is the one."

Samuel anointed David and the spirit of God entered David.

God left Saul, and an evil spirit entered him, tormenting him.

Saul's servants said, "Behold, an evil spirit from God is in you. Send us to find a man skilful at the lyre. When badly tormented, he will play and calm you."

"Go," said Saul. "Find such a man."

"There is one, the son of Jesse of Bethlehem," said one young servant. "He is skilful."

Saul sent for David, and David came and entered his service. Saul loved him greatly and he became Saul's armour bearer.

Saul asked Jesse to let David stay.

Whenever God sent the evil spirit to torment Saul, the boy David would play the lyre and the evil spirit would depart.

David Meets Goliath

David was a shepherd, the youngest son of Jesse of Bethlehem.

Saul the king of Israel was at war with the Philistines.

The army of the Philistines stood on one mountain and Saul and the Israelites stood on another.

One morning, a man strode out of the Philistine army to stand before the Israelites. He was the tallest and strongest man any had ever seen. He was Goliath of Gath. He stood and shouted to the Israelite army, "Why have you come to do battle? Choose one from amongst you to come out to fight me. If he fights me and kills me, we will be your servants, but if I win you will all be our servants."

When Saul and his army heard these words, they were dismayed and afraid. Who could fight such a man and win?

David was caring for the sheep in the hills, but three of his brothers were in the Israelite army. Jesse sent David down to where the army was camped with loaves of bread for his brothers.

"Find them, and give me some word of how they are," Jesse told David.

David reached the army camp, and ran to the ranks where his brothers were. He greeted them warmly and was asking after them when Goliath came out of the ranks of the Philistine army to give his daily challenge. David heard him, and he saw the soldiers of Israel run before him.

"Have you seen him?" they asked David. "Surely whoever goes against him will be given great riches by the King."

"Whoever kills this Philistine kills someone who defies the armies of the living God," answered David.

David's brothers heard his words. "You don't know what you're talking about. "Anyway, if you're here, who's looking after the sheep? Are you only here to see a battle?"

"What did I say wrong?" asked David, and he asked the same question of the other soldiers.

David's words soon reached Saul's ears and he sent for David.

"I will fight this Philistine," David told Saul.

"You cannot fight the Philistine," said Saul. "You are but a boy, and he has been a soldier since he was a boy."

"I kept sheep for my father," David said. "And I killed lions and even bears that dared to take lambs from the flock. This Philistine is just like a bear, and I have killed many of them. He should not be allowed to say what he does against our God. God will help me as he helped me against the lions and the bears."

Saul had David dressed in armour and a sword buckled to his side. However, David was not used to these things, and said, "Take these off. I cannot move in them, let alone fight. I will use what I always use."

With that he picked up five smooth stones from a nearby brook. He already carried his sling.

He then walked up to where the Philistine still stood, challenging the Israelite army.

Goliath looked on David with disdain. "Is this what they send out? Are you going to throw sticks for me then? Come here and I shall leave your body to the birds of the air!"

"You come with sword and spear," David shouted at Goliath, "but I come with my God with me. Today, the lord will deliver you to my hand, and I will cut off your head. It will be your body left to the birds and animals. Today the world will know of the God of Israel."

The ranks of the Philistine army straightened up at the challenge, and stood behind their champion Goliath.

Goliath strode out in front to meet David.

David took one of the pebbles, and put it quickly in the sling. The sling whirled around his head, and Goliath smiled to see such a puny weapon.

The stone flew out of the sling and hit Goliath on his forehead, sinking into his face. Goliath dropped onto his face on the ground, the smile gone.

David ran over to Goliath, and with Goliath's own sword struck off the Philistine's head.

When the Philistines saw that Goliath, their champion, was dead they fled from the battlefield. The armies of Israel jumped up, and pursued the Philistines, chasing them far away.

David took the head of the Philistine to Saul. From then on, David was the champion of the Israelite army and loved by everyone. One day, he would be King.

David the Outlaw

After killing the giant Goliath, David was taken to King Saul and met Jonathan, his son.

Jonathan immediately loved David as a brother, and gave him his armour and weapons.

Saul grew to hate David, and David knew that Saul would try to kill him.

He spoke to Jonathan. "Your father will try to kill me. Tomorrow there will be feasting. Tell your father that I have returned to Jerusalem. If he is angry you'll know he hates me."

The two youths went to the fields.

"Hide behind that pile of stones. I will come shooting with my bow," said Jonathan. "If you must flee, I'll tell the boy fetching the arrows to look further on. If it is safe I'll tell him to look this side of him."

At the feast, Saul asked after David and was furious to hear he had gone away.

"As long as David is alive, you will never be king!" Saul shouted at Jonathan.

Jonathan left, and the next morning he went shooting.

"Run for the arrows," he told the lad with him, and he shot the arrows far beyond him. "The arrows are beyond you, boy."

David came out of his hiding place.

"You must go," said Jonathan. "Go in peace. Our families will always be enemies."

David left and Jonathan returned to the city.

Israel's New King

After David left Jonathan, he went to the village of Nob to see the priest, Ahimelech.

"The king, Saul, has commanded us to do certain matters, but we need some food," he told the priest.

"There is some holy bread," said the priest.

"And I left so quickly on Saul's business, I came without sword or arms," added David.

"There is Goliath's sword, here, on the altar," said Ahimelech.

"There is no sword like it," said David. "I will take it."

Unfortunately, the conversation was overheard by Doeg, a servant of Saul's. He hurried to tell Saul. Saul immediately ordered the death of everyone of Nob.

David had meanwhile gathered a small army. One of the sons of Ahimelech escaped from the village and reached David's camp, telling him of the murders.

"Stay with me and you will be

56

safe," David told the young man.

David took a small army to Engedi, and hid deep in the caves.

Saul learned that David was at Engedi, and took his army there.

Saul went into the cave where David was hiding and David was able to creep up to him and cut off part of Saul's skirt.

"Kill him," David's men told him.

"No, I cannot," said David. "He is still the anointed king."

Saul then left the cave, and David followed him out and called out to Saul.

"Why do you believe I would kill you?" he asked Saul. "I could have killed you moments ago, but I did not and I will not sin against you."

Saul was ashamed. "You have repaid my evil with good. I know surely that you will be King of Israel one day. Swear that you will not kill my descendants."

David swore this, and was true to his word, for it was the Philistines who killed Saul and his sons.

Solomon Becomes King

King David was old, and had reigned for many years. He had many sons, but had promised Bathsheba that her son, Solomon, would be king of Israel after him.

David's son, Adonijah, decided that it was time he became king.

"I will be King," he told Joab and Abiathar the priest. He gathered chariots and horsemen.

Nathan the prophet was not with Adonijah, and he spoke to Bathsheba.

"Adonijah says he will be King, and David does not realise it," he said. "You must speak to David. I will support you."

Bathsheba went to the king and bowed before him.

"My lord," began Bathsheba. "You swore to me by the Lord God, that Solomon, my son, will reign after you. And behold, Adonijah is King, although you do not know it. He has made sacrifices and has invited your other sons to join him. Now all the eyes of Israel are upon you to see who you shall name to be the next King."

Nathan the prophet came in while Bathsheba was talking.

Nathan asked the same question. "Have you said that Adonijah will reign after you and that he will sit upon your throne? For he has made sacrifices today and is feasting with your other sons. Zadok the priest, myself and Solomon are not invited. Have you made a decision and not told us?"

"Bring back Bathsheba," said David.

When Bathsheba returned, David said, "I swore to you by the Lord, that Solomon, your son, shall reign in Israel after me. We will arrange it today."

"May you rule forever," said Bathsheba, as she bowed to the ground.

"Call the priest," said David. "Arrange for Solomon to ride my mule to Gihon, and let Zadok and Nathan proclaim him King over Israel. Blow the trumpet and call, 'Long Live King Solomon!' Then seat him on a throne for he shall be King in my place. I appoint him ruler over Israel and Judah."

"Amen!" declared the priest and prophet.

So Zadok and Nathan did as David commanded in Gihon, and Solomon was proclaimed King.

The townspeople rejoiced and the noise reached Adonijah as he was feasting. He and his guests soon heard the news that David had proclaimed Solomon the next king.

Adonijah's guests trembled at the news and then each left and went his own way.

Solomon's Wisdom

Solomon was the son of King David and he loved God a great deal. God appeared to Solomon one night in a dream.

"Ask what I shall give you," God said to Solomon.

"You showed great love to my father, and gave him a son to sit on his throne. I am that son and you have made me king of a great people. Therefore give me an understanding mind to govern the people. Let me tell

between good and evil."

God was pleased with Solomon's answer. "You did not ask for anything for yourself - neither long life nor riches, but to be able to tell what is right. Behold I give you a wise and discerning mind."

Two women were brought before Solomon.

"My lord, this woman and I live in the same house," one of the women told Solomon. "She was in the house on the day that I gave birth to my baby. Then three days later, she had her baby. We were in the house alone. In the night her baby son died, and at midnight she came to my room. She took my living baby from me, and put her dead baby in its place. I awoke in the morning to find the dead baby. I was most upset, but I looked closer. I saw that it was not my baby."

"The living child is mine," said the other woman. "Yours is dead."

"You lie," cried the first woman. "The living child is mine."

And so the two women argued before the king.

Solomon held up his hands to silence them.

"One of you says 'the living child is mine and the dead child yours' and the other says 'no, your son is dead and mine is living.'"

He sat back and called for a sword.

"Now, the living child shall be cut in two halves. You shall both have half each of the living child."

The mother of the child could not bear to see this done. "No!" she cried.

"Give her the baby. Please don't kill him."

The mother of the dead child said, "Divide it, then it is neither hers nor mine."

Solomon passed the sword back to the guard.

"Give the living child to the first woman. Do not kill the boy. She is his mother."

All Israel heard of the judgement and marvelled at the wisdom of the king.

Elisha and the Syrians

The King of the Syrians was making war on Israel. He told his servants one day to make camp in a certain place.

God sent word to Elisha.

"Do not send the army near to this place," Elisha warned the King of Israel. The army was therefore saved from attack.

The King of Syria was greatly troubled at this.

"Is there a spy for the King of Israel among us?" he asked his servants.

"No, my lord," they replied. "But Elisha, who is prophet to the King of Israel seems to hear all that is said in your bedchamber."

"Go, seize him," said the King. "Bring him here."

A great army was sent, and it surrounded Elisha's city at night.

Elisha awoke early next morning, and saw the great army surrounding the city.

"Master! What shall we do?" exclaimed Elisha's young servant.

"Fear not, for those who are with us are more than those against us,"

Elisha said, and then prayed, "O Lord, open his eyes that he might see."

The Lord opened the young man's eyes, so that he saw the mountain was full of horses and chariots of fire around Elisha.

The Syrians attacked, and Elisha prayed. "Strike them blind!" And they were struck blind.

Elisha went out to them. "This is not the way, or the city. I will take you to the man. Follow me."

Elisha led the Syrian army to Samaria. There he asked God to restore their sight. The King of Israel saw them.

"Shall I slay them?" he asked.

"No," said Elisha. "Would you kill those captured in battle? Feed them and return them to their master."

A great feast was prepared, and when it was over the army left. The Syrians stopped their raids on the land of Israel.

A Warrior is Cured

Naaman was the commander of the Syrian army and was highly favoured by the King, but Naaman was also a leper.

On one raid, a young Israeli girl was taken, and she was now a handmaiden to Naaman's wife.

She loved her mistress and told her, "Would that your husband could meet the prophet Elisha. He would cure him of his leprosy."

Naaman told his king of the girl's words.

The king sent Naaman with a letter to the King of Israel. Naaman took much gold and silver.

Elisha heard of the visitor, and went to the king. "Let him come to me so that he may know there is a prophet in Israel."

Naaman went to Elisha's house, and Elisha sent out a messenger with

instructions.

"Go and wash in the Jordan seven times, and you will be cured," said the messenger.

But Naaman was angry. "I thought he would come out and wave his hands over me! Syrian rivers are just as good! Can I not wash there and be cured?"

He turned away in a rage, but his servants approached him. "If he had told you to do a great thing, wouldn't you have done it? Instead he says 'Wash and be clean'."

So Naaman went to the Jordan and washed seven times, and he was cured, his flesh restored like a child's.

He returned to Elisha's house, determined to give him the gold and silver, but Elisha refused to accept the gift.

"Let me take some soil to build an altar in my home," said Naaman. "And even though I go to our temple I will pray to your god."

"Go in peace," said Elisha.

Naaman left, and was swiftly followed by Gehazi, a servant of Elisha. Naaman dismounted when he saw him.

"My Master sends me. Two prophets have arrived, and he asks if you will give some silver," said Gehazi.

Gehazi returned to his home with the silver and hid it. He returned to his master.

"Gehazi, I was with you in spirit when you met with Naaman," said Elisha.

"Therefore you and your descendants will inherit his leprosy."

And Gehazi left as a leper.

Daniel in the Lion's Den

Daniel, of the tribe of Judah, was a prisoner of the Babylonians.

Darius became King of Babylon, and admired Daniel greatly. He made him governor of part of the kingdom. The other governors were very jealous and plotted ways to make him fall from favour.

Daniel governed well, and the other governors could find no fault with him.

"The only way we can find complaint against Daniel is in connection with his God," decided the governors.

They approached Darius with a proclamation.

"O, King Darius. All the governors and counsellors agree that you should issue a proclamation that no god or man should be worshipped for thirty days except for the King. Any who break the law will be thrown to the lions."

King Darius signed the document.

Daniel heard of this new law, but still prayed at his window in the direction of Jerusalem three times a day.

The other governors knew of this and went to Darius.

"Did you not sign a law forbidding the worship of any god or man for thirty days, with the punishment of being thrown to the lions?" they asked.

"I did," answered Darius.

"That Daniel ignores your law," the governors told Darius.

Darius was upset to hear this. He admired Daniel, and all day tried to change the punishment but the

governors would not have it.

"Daniel has broken your law, and must be punished," they said. "You cannot change a law once you have signed it."

Darius called for Daniel.

"You must be thrown in with the lions," Darius told Daniel. "May your God be with you."

Daniel was sent into the den, and the opening was sealed behind him.

Darius returned to his palace, worrying all night about the fate of Daniel.

At first light he was back at the cave, demanding the den be opened.

"Daniel," he called. "Did your God deliver you?"

Quietly did Daniel answer him.

"O, King, my God sent his angels to shut the mouths of the lions because I was innocent before him and before you."

Darius was glad. Daniel was brought out of the den and there was not one mark on him.

Darius ordered that those who had falsely accused Daniel be thrown in with the lions.

Darius ordered a new decree, that Daniel's god was the living God, and should be feared in all his kingdom.

A Whale Swallows Jonah

God appeared before Jonah. "Go to Nineveh, and tell the people I know their wicked ways."

Jonah was scared and he ran. He took a ship to Tarshish, hoping to escape God.

God created a great storm and the ship was hurled from wave to wave. The sailors drew lots to see who was the cause of the evil, and Jonah was chosen.

"Who are you?" they demanded.

"I am a Hebrew, trying to escape from my God."

"How can we calm the sea?" cried the sailors, as the storm grew stronger.

"Throw me into the sea," said Jonah. "The sea will grow calm. It is my fault the storm has gripped your ship."

The sailors still tried to control the ship, unwilling to throw a man overboard, but the storm worsened.

Finally, they called out to God, "We beg you not to let us die because of this man, and do not condemn us for casting him overboard." They then threw Jonah out into the waves, and the sea calmed down instantly.

A whale swallowed Jonah, and for the next three days and nights Jonah lived in its belly.

Then Jonah prayed, asking for God's forgiveness.

God spoke to the whale and the whale took Jonah to the shore.

God told Jonah again to go to Nineveh.

"Tell them I know they are wicked. They must repent or I will destroy the city in forty days."

Jonah went into the city, giving the people God's message.

The people listened, and put aside their wicked ways. All people, from the king down, wore sackcloth, and repented.

God saw their repentance, and did not punish them for their city's wickedness.

Jonah was angry that the city was spared after all he had endured, and went out of the city.

God made a tall plant grow overnight to give Jonah shade in the heat of the day. Jonah was pleased to have the plant. But next day God made a worm attack the plant and kill it, taking away Jonah's shade for the hot day.

In the severe heat, Jonah begged to die.

"Do you pity the plant?" God asked him. "You did not make it grow in one night, and let it die the next. Should I not therefore pity Nineveh?"

The Birth of Jesus

A decree went out from Jerusalem - all people of Israel were to be counted. Everyone was to return to the city of their birth.

Joseph was a carpenter. He and his wife Mary were to return from Nazareth to Bethlehem. Mary was expecting a baby and she had been told by the angel Gabriel that the baby was the son of God and should be called Jesus.

When they arrived at Bethlehem, they could find nowhere to stay except for the stables of an inn.

Mary had her baby there, and he was wrapped in swaddling clothes and put in a manger for a cradle.

There were shepherds guarding sheep in the fields around Bethlehem, and as they watched over them a golden light suddenly shone around them.

"What is it?" they cried, scared at the sound of singing and bright light.

There appeared before them an angel, shining brightly.

"Be not afraid," said the angel. "I bring glad tidings, for you and all men. Tonight a baby is born in the town of Bethlehem, and he is the saviour. You

will find him in swaddling clothes lying in a manger."

Suddenly there was a host of angels and they sang and sang.

"Let us go to Bethlehem and find the baby," said the shepherds, and they made their way to the small town.

They saw a star shining over a stable, and entering they saw the ass and the oxen, and also Mary and Joseph. There, in the manger, lay the baby as the angel had told them. They told all people how they knew the baby had been born.

Three kings from distant lands had been studying the skies and heavens for many years, and knew that a great king was to be born. They each followed a bright star and met at the edge of a desert.

"I'm following this star to the birth of a king," said one Melchior.

The other two kings, Gaspar and Balthasar realised that they were also following the same star, and the three

decided to travel together.

They arrived in Jerusalem and asked to see the new king. "He has been born king of the Jews, and we have seen his star in the east," the kings told Herod.

"When you find the king, tell me where he is," said Herod, much troubled by the news of a new king. "I will go to worship him."

The three kings eventually reached the town of Bethlehem and saw the star high above the stable. The people and the shepherds stood back at their approach.

They went in and immediately saw the baby in the manger.

"This is the king, the saviour," they cried, and they gave their gifts of gold, myrrh and frankincense.

They would have returned to Jerusalem, but a dream from God told them to go straight home.

Joseph also had a dream. "Take Mary and the baby Jesus and flee to Egypt. Stay there until I tell you to return. Herod is about to search for the child to destroy him."

Joseph left that night, taking Mary and the baby.

Herod realised that the kings were not returning to Jerusalem, and he sent orders to Bethlehem that all male children, two years and under, be killed.

Joseph and Mary stayed in Egypt until Herod was dead. Then an angel appeared before Joseph. "Return to the land of Israel. Those who sought the death of the child are dead.

Joseph and Mary returned, and went to live in Nazareth.

The Childhood of Jesus

Jesus grew to boyhood in Nazareth. He was a happy and wise boy, and God was with him.

Mary and Joseph went to Jerusalem every year to celebrate the Passover, as was the custom. When Jesus was twelve years old, they went as usual, taking Jesus with them.

When all the feasting was finished, Mary and Joseph left Jerusalem for home, travelling with many friends. They presumed that Jesus was travelling with some of his friends, somewhere else in the group.

Evening came, and the group stopped for the night. Jesus did not appear.

"Where is he?" Mary asked Joseph.

They asked among their friends. "Has anyone seen Jesus?"

"No, we've not seen him since we left Jerusalem," replied his friends. Mary and Joseph searched, but could not find the twelve-year old Jesus.

They were very concerned, and turned back for Jerusalem.

They searched for three days, and then finally found him at the temple.

He was sitting among the teachers, listening and asking questions.

All who heard him were amazed at his understanding and knowledge.

Mary and Joseph went up the steps of the temple.

"My son!" cried Mary. "Your father and I have been looking for you. We were worried. How could you do this?"

"But mother, I don't understand. Why should you be so worried?" said Jesus. "Where else would I be but in my Father's house?"

Joseph and Mary did not understand what he said, but Jesus returned to Nazareth with them, and was obedient to them. He continued to grow in God's favour, and grew in wisdom and years.

Jesus Gathers his Disciples

Jesus began to preach, but knew that he needed helpers. He was walking by the Sea of Galilee and he saw two men.

The two brothers, Simon and Andrew, were fishermen and were about to cast their net into the sea.

"Come with me," Jesus said to them, "and I will make you fishers of men."

They both immediately left their net and followed Jesus.

Jesus later changed Simon's name to Peter.

Going on from there, he saw two

other brothers, James and John, the sons of Zebedee. They were on the beach, mending their fishing nets. Jesus called to them and they followed him as well.

The next day, Jesus was at Bethsaida and he found a man named Philip.

"Come with me," Jesus said to Philip.

Philip found his friend Bartholomew and told him, "I have found the man the prophets spoke of. He is Jesus, the son of Joseph of Nazareth."

Jesus then came to Nazareth and saw a tax-collector quarrelling with some men.

"Come, Matthew," said Jesus. "Come with me."

And Matthew left his work and followed.

Jesus gathered twelve disciples to him and they were Simon, known as Peter, his brother Andrew, James and John, Philip and Bartholomew, Matthew and Thomas, James the son of Alphaeus, Simon, Judas the son of James and Judas Iscariot, who was to betray Jesus.

The twelve apostles went everywhere with Jesus, learning from him, healing the sick, preaching and baptising the followers.

Jesus and the Children

esus was at Capernaum when the disciples came to him with a question. "Who is the greatest in heaven?" they asked.

Jesus called to a small child that was at the front of the crowd surrounding him and the disciples. He held him out in front of the disciples.

"Unless you become like children you will never enter the kingdom of heaven.

"Whoever is humble like this child

will be the greatest in heaven. Whoever makes a child sin will never enter the kingdom of heaven. All these little ones are very precious to my Father."

Some time later, Jesus left Galilee and went into the region of Judea. Again large crowds followed him and the disciples, and he healed the sick there and taught and spoke of God.

One day, he was talking to the Pharisees and his disciples in front of a large crowd of people, when some children were brought up to him.

"Please lay your hands on our children," the parents asked of Jesus, carrying their small children in their arms or holding the older ones in front of them.

The disciples jumped up to move the people back to the crowd.

"Come now," said the disciples, moving the children and their families before them. "Jesus is talking, and it is very important. He doesn't have time to see the children now."

"Stop," said Jesus, standing up. "Let the children come close. Do not prevent them from coming to me. The kingdom of heaven belongs to such as these."

He held the small babies, and laid his hands on all the children before him, and then he left.

Calming the Storm

Jesus was preaching and healing the sick. He went to his disciple Peter's house and healed Peter's mother-in-law who was lying ill in bed. He touched her hand and the fever left her.

That evening many people came, bringing friends and relatives who were sick. They left cured and well. Jesus saw that the crowds were becoming larger and larger, and decided to leave.

"Come, we will take a boat to the other side of the sea," Jesus told his disciples.

Jesus and the disciples boarded a boat, and started to cross the sea. Jesus slept on a cushion in the stern.

As he slept, a great storm began. Huge waves threatened to swamp the boat. The fierce wind was blowing them in all directions and the boat was impossible to steer.

The disciples were terrified and woke Jesus, who was sleeping through the uproar. "Save us!" they cried. "The boat will sink!"

"Why are you afraid?" asked Jesus, and he stood and spoke calmly to the wind and rain. The storm died.

The disciples marvelled at a man who could control even the wind and seas.

The Sermon on the Mount

Jesus went about Galilee, teaching in the synagogues and preaching the gospel. He healed the sick of all diseases. His fame spread through all Syria and people brought friends and family who were ill with various diseases, or who were in great pain. They brought those who were paralysed, or lepers, and Jesus healed them all.

Great crowds followed him from Galilee and Decapolis, Jerusalem and Judea and from beyond the river Jordan.

Jesus saw the growing crowds of people following him and climbed part way up the slope of a mountain. His disciples sat down with him and he began to talk to them. He told them many things.

"Blessed are the meek and gentle, for they will inherit the earth," he said.

"Blessed are the poor in spirit, for the kingdom of Heaven is theirs," he said.

"Blessed are the pure in heart, for they shall see God," he said.

"When you light a lamp, you do not hide it under a cover, or put it under a bed, you put it on a stand so that it gives light to all the people in the room. Therefore, let your light shine before all men so that all your good works are seen," Jesus told the disciples.

"When you pray, do not shout it from the street corners, but go to your room and pray quietly. God will still hear you and will quietly reward you.

"Do not worry about food and clothing. You see the birds in the air - they do not plant or reap and sow, or collect food in barns, but God still makes sure they are fed. Also look at the lilies in the field. They do not work or spin, and yet Solomon in his most magnificent clothing was never as beautiful as one of these. So do not be anxious about these things for God will provide these when you seek his kingdom."

Jesus told the people many things, and when he was finished the people were astonished at the way he spoke, for it was as a teacher with authority and not as one of the scribes who had only read the scriptures.

Jesus then came down from the mountain and crowds still followed him. A leper knelt before him.

"Lord, if you want to, you can make me well," the leper said.

Jesus stretched out his hand and touched him. "I want to, you are clean." At once the man's leprosy was cured.

"Say nothing to anybody," Jesus told the leper. "Go and show yourself to the priest."

The Stories Jesus Told

Jesus went about the land, preaching God's word. One day, he told the story about the good Samaritan.

One day, a man was travelling from Jerusalem to Jericho. He was attacked by thieves, who stripped him, beat him and left him for dead. Later that day, a priest travelled the same road. He saw the man lying in the road and passed by on the other side. A Levite passed on the same road and crossed the road to avoid the man lying there. Some time later, a Samaritan came to the place in the road and saw the man. His heart was full of pity for him. He took him to a nearby inn. The next day he took some money and gave it to the innkeeper.

"Take care of the poor man," said the Samaritan. "If you spend more money than this, I will repay you on my return."

"Which of these three people was a neighbour to the traveller who was attacked?" Jesus asked his listeners.

"The one who showed mercy," answered one.

"Then go and do likewise," Jesus said to him.

Jesus told his listeners the story of the prodigal son. "There was a man who had two sons. The younger man went to his father and

84

said, "Father, give me my portion of my inheritance that I may go out into the world."

His father did as his son requested, and put together a sum that was equal to his inheritance.

A few days later, the young man left his home taking all his belongings and his inheritance with him.

He settled in a distant land and squandered all his fortune in loose living. He didn't save a penny. When he had spent all his money, a great famine took over that country, and the young

man found that he would have to work to live.

He found a job as a swineherd. He would gladly have eaten the food the swine were given, but nobody gave him food.

"My father feeds his servants better," said the young man. "If I stay here I will starve. I will return to my father and say: 'I have sinned before heaven and before you. I am no longer worthy to be your son. Please take me on as a servant.'"

The young man left the swine and returned to his homeland. While he was still a short way from the house, his father saw him. He went running to greet his son. He threw his arms around him and kissed him.

"Father, I have sinned against you and heaven," said the young man, hanging his head. "I am not worthy to be called your son."

"Hush, son," said the father. He called to his servants to bring the best robe.

"Put it on my son, and put shoes on his feet."

He called to the other servants to kill the fatted calf.

"We must eat and make merry. My son was dead and is alive again. He was lost and is found."

The older son was working in the field, and suddenly heard music coming from the house. He called to his servant.

"What is the meaning of this music?"

"Your brother has returned, and your father has killed the fatted calf, because he has returned safely."

The older brother was angry and would not go into the house.

His father came to speak to him. "Please come, my son, and make merry with us."

"I have served you for many years," said the older son. "You have never killed so much as a young goat for me and my friends and yet my brother has thrown away his inheritance on wild living, and you welcome him with open arms and kill the fatted calf for him!"

"My son," said his father. "You are

always with me and all that is mine will one day be yours. Should I not be glad that your brother was dead and is alive, was lost and is found?"

"There is great joy in heaven," Jesus told his listeners, "in one sinner who repents."

A man called his servants. To one he gave five talents, to the second two talents, and to the third one talent. He then went away.

The servant who received five talents traded and soon earned five more. The servant who received two talents did the same and earned two more.

But the third servant dug a hole and buried his master's money.

After a time, the man returned.

"Master, you gave me five talents and I have made five more," said the first servant.

"Well done, good and faithful servant," said the man.

"You gave me two talents," said the second servant, "and I have made two more."

"Well done," said his master.

The third servant approached. "Master, I knew you were a hard man, and I was afraid, so I buried your talent. Here it is."

His master was angry. "You stupid servant. You should have invested my money and returned it with interest. Therefore give your talent to the man who has made more of his."

The Wonders of Jesus

Lazarus of Bethany was ill. His sisters, Mary and Martha went to Jesus.

"Lord, our brother is ill," they said.

Jesus told them. "He will not die."

Even though Lazarus was ill, Jesus stayed where he was. After two days, he said, "Lazarus sleeps. I will go to wake him."

"If he sleeps, he will recover," said the disciples.

"Lazarus is dead," said Jesus. "I was not there, so now you may believe."

Jesus returned to Bethany to hear that Lazarus had died, and had been in his tomb for four days.

Martha met Jesus. "If you had been here, Lord, he would not have died."

"He will live again," Jesus told Martha and went to the tomb. A stone covered the doorway.

"Take away the stone," said Jesus. As the stone was moved, Jesus prayed.

"Father, let those that hear me believe you sent me."

Then he called out in a loud voice. "Lazarus, come out!"

And Lazarus stepped out of the tomb, wrapped head to foot in bandages.

"Unbind him," said Jesus.

Lazarus was well, and many of the people that were with Jesus now believed.

Jesus was travelling around the country, teaching the people and healing the sick.

He travelled to the Sea of Galilee, through the region of Decapolis. There a deaf and dumb man was brought to him.

"Please lay your hand on him," the man's relatives pleaded to Jesus.

Jesus took the deaf man's ears and touched his tongue.

Jesus looked up. "Be opened," he said.

And the man's ears were opened so that he could hear, and his tongue was freed so he could speak. He spoke as if he had been speaking all his life.

"Tell no one of this," Jesus said.

But the people were so amazed and astonished they told everyone they met.

"He can make even the deaf to hear and the dumb to speak!" they declared.

Jesus was on his way to Jerusalem. It was as he was passing between Samaria and Galilee, that he entered a village and saw ten lepers standing on the edge of the village, away from the house.

They saw Jesus coming, and called to him as loudly as they could.

"Master!" they cried from a distance. "Master, have mercy on us!" They dare not come any closer because of their leprosy.

"Go and show yourselves to the priests," Jesus told the lepers. And the men turned to go.

As they walked away, towards the temple, each of the lepers was cured.

They stared at each other in amazement

"We're well again!" they cried. And they hugged each other, delighted and astonished that their leprosy was gone.

One of them looked back. "I must thank the man who did this!" he declared, and he headed back to the entrance of the village. Jesus was still there.

The man threw himself at Jesus' feet, praising God in a loud voice. The man was a Samaritan, and not of Israel.

"Ten lepers were cured, weren't they?" said Jesus. "Where are the other nine? Could none of them return to give thanks and praise to God for their cure, except for this Samaritan?"

Jesus helped the man to stand.

"Rise," he said. "Go your way in peace. It is your faith that has made you well."

Jesus was in Jerusalem with the disciples. They passed a row of beggars, leaning against a wall. One of the beggars had been blind since birth.

Jesus stopped and looked at the man. He then spat on the ground and made clay with the dirt. He picked up this clay and called to the blind man. He then carefully put the clay over the blind man's closed eyes.

"Go to the Pool of Siloam," Jesus said to the blind man. "Wash your face and eyes in the water there."

The man went to the pool, washed his eyes and found that he could see. He hurried back to his begging place.

The beggars who had sat near the blind man looked on in astonishment. "Isn't this the blind man who usually sits with us and begs?"

"Yes, it is," said some, peering at the man.

"No," said some of the others. "It is not. This man just looks like him."

"It is me," said the man.

"How can you see?" asked his friends.

"The man called Jesus put clay on my eyes and told me to wash in the Pool at Siloam. I did as he said and now I can see," said the man.

"Where is he now?" asked the beggars.

"I do not know," said the man. "I believe he must be a prophet."

Jairus was a leader of the synagogue. When Jesus came to his city Jairus went to him.

"Please come to my house," he

pleaded. "My only daughter is dying."

Jesus went with Jairus, and as he went people pressed about him. A woman who had been ill for twelve years and could not be cured, came up behind Jesus and touched his cloak. She was immediately cured.

Jesus stopped and asked, "Who touched me?"

"There is a crowd," said Peter. "Anyone could have touched you."

"Someone touched me and power has gone from me," replied Jesus.

The woman realised that it was she, and knelt down. "I touched you and was healed," she said.

"Your faith healed you," said Jesus. "Go in peace."

At that moment a man from Jairus' house arrived. "Do not trouble the teacher," he told Jairus. "Your daughter has just died."

Jesus heard. "Fear not," he said. "She will be well."

At the house, all were crying for the dead girl.

"Do not cry," said Jesus to her

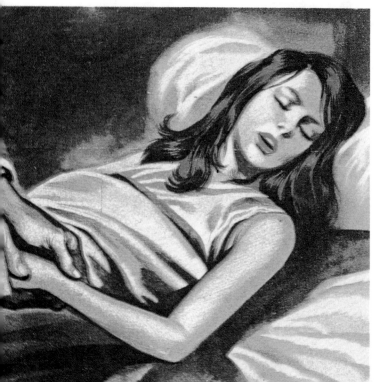

parents. "She is sleeping." He then took her hand, saying, "Child, arise."

The girl stood up at once.

"Give her something to eat," Jesus told her astonished parents. "And tell no one what has happened."

Jesus went to the Sea of Galilee, and a great crowd of men, women and children followed. They had seen the miracles Jesus had performed on those who were ill.

Jesus saw the great number that followed, and went up into the hills. He sat down with his disciples. He then looked out over the great crowd of people that had followed them and were now gathered there, waiting. He turned to Philip.

"Well, Philip, how shall we buy enough bread to feed all these people? They are probably very hungry by now." Jesus asked the question, but he already knew what he would have to do.

Philip looked at the great crowd and sighed. "Two hundred denari would not buy enough bread to give each person even a little!" he declared.

Andrew was standing close by. "There is a young lad here with five barley loaves and two fish," he said, counting the items in the boy's basket. "But that's not going to be much use when there are so many people."

"Tell the people to sit down," said Jesus, standing up.

The disciples quickly told the people at the front of the crowd to sit, and the message was passed back

through the multitude until eventually all were seated.

They numbered five thousand people there, sitting on the grass.

Jesus then took the basket of loaves and fish from the young boy. He looked up to heaven and then blessed the loaves and fish, giving thanks. He then shared them out to all the men, women and children who were seated there. Each person was able to eat as much as he or she wanted.

When everyone had eaten their fill, Jesus said to the disciples, "Take a basket each and go among the people. Gather up all the food that is left over, so that nothing is wasted."

The disciples then each took a basket and filled it to the brim with the leftover bread and fish. The crowd of people gasped when they saw twelve full baskets of food. These were the remains from five barley loaves and two fish.

The people saw this miracle and cried out, "Here is our king."

Jesus quickly went into the hills to be alone.